WELCOME!

We are passionate about marriage and this couple's journal was borne out of our desire to create an opportunity for couples to learn and grow in their love for each other and God.

Journaling together draws you closer as a couple and helps to bring your goals, hopes and dreams alive. We hope that this will be a wonderful way for you to thank God for your of marriage and share your appreciation for one another.

Our journaling journey has been a source of great encouragement to us as we have seen hopes, dreams and ideas come to fruition. We are also aware of hopes, dreams and prayers yet unfulfilled and journaling has helped us to keep our focus whilst trusting God.

There are a variety of ways you can use this Journal. We have chosen a weekly format and each week has a topic, scripture and reflection point. This gives you an opportunity to share and write your collective thoughts.

Before you start we would like you to take time out to discuss what you both hope to accomplish, include things that are most important to you both.
This is your keepsake so we encourage you to personalise it by adding photos, cards and any other items that you want to remember.

Our prayer for you is that as you read the scriptures together,the Holy Spirit will in-spire your thoughts, the scriptures will come alive and God will share His heart, plans and purposes for you as a couple.

We would like to encourage you to use the companion Seeds of Love Couples Devotional with this Journal.

Please also share your love stories with us at
seedsoflove@lovetalks.tv

Follow us on Twitter, Facebook and Instagram (@Lovetalkstv)
May God bless and preserve your marriage.
In His love and ours,

Kemi and Bode Olutunbi

To:

From:

Date:

WEEK ONE

God's Design for Marriage

Genesis 2:18-25

Heart to heart: In what ways do you need to accept your spouse as a gift to you?

WEEK TWO

Marriage: A Safe Haven

Isaiah 32:2

Heart to heart: What do you need from your spouse to experience a safe haven marriage?

WEEK THREE

A Vision for your Marriage

Habbakuk 2:2

Heart to heart: How are you working as a team to fulfil God's vision for your marriage?

WEEK FOUR

Sex: A Divine Gift (Part 1)

Song of Solomon 7:1-9

Heart to heart: How can you make your sex life more fulfilling?

WEEK FIVE

Sex: A Divine Gift (Part 2)

1 Corinthinans 7:2-5

Heart to heart: What is your attitude towards sex. Is there anything holding you back from fully enjoying sex?

WEEK SIX

The Gift of Oneness

Genesis 2:24-25

Heart to heart: Are there ways in which you are drifting away from each other and not embracing the gift of oneness in your marriage? How can you stop this drift?

WEEK SEVEN

Loving Your Wife

I Peter 3:7

Heart to heart: Ask your wife what loving her means to her. In what ways can you show love to her this week?

WEEK EIGHT

Honouring Your Husband

I Peter 3:1-2

Heart to heart: Ask your husband what honouring him means to him. In what ways can you honour him this week?

WEEK NINE

A Mutual Responsibility to Love

Ephesians 5:21,25-29

Heart to heart (Husband): In what ways can you show sacrificial leadership?
Heart to heart (Wife): In what ways can you show submission?

WEEK TEN

God's Plan for Your Marriage

Jeremiah 29:11

Heart to heart: What do you know about God's plan for your marriage?

WEEK ELEVEN

Pillars of a Successful Marriage
Cleaving

Genesis 2:24

Heart to heart: What can you do to cleave more closely to each other?

WEEK TWELVE

Pillars of a Successful Marriage

Choosing Oneness

Genesis 2:24

Heart to heart: In what ways can you actively pursue oneness in your marriage?

WEEK THIRTEEN

Pillars of a Successful Marriage
Naked and Unashamed

Genesis 2:24

Heart to heart: What steps can you take to be more vulnerable with each other?

WEEK FOURTEEN

Pillars of a Successful Marriage
Intimacy (Part 1)

Genesis 2:25

Heart to heart: What can you do to communicate better with each other?

WEEK FIFTEEN

Pillars of a Successful Marriage
Intimacy (Part 2)

Genesis 2:25

Heart to heart: In what ways can you increase emotional, physical and spiritual intimacy in your marriage?

WEEK SIXTEEN

Pillars of a Successful Marriage Intimacy (Part 3)

Genesis 2:25

Heart to heart: What steps do you need to take to foster a safe environment for open and honest communication in your relationship?

WEEK SEVENTEEN

Listening
The Way to Your Wife's Heart

James 1:19

Heart to heart: Ask your wife to share the things you can do to make her feel listened to.

WEEK EIGHTEEN

Pillars of a Successful Marriage

Respect: The Way to Your Husband's Heart

I Peter 3:2

Heart to heart: Are your words or tone of voice showing respect to your husband?

WEEK NINETEEN

Loving Against All Odds

Philippians 2:4

Heart to heart: In what ways can you build your (phileo) friendship in your marriage?

WEEK TWENTY

Your Number One Priority

John 15:13

Heart to heart: How can you demonstrate that you are each other's priority this week?

WEEK TWENTY ONE

Protecting Your Marriage (Part 1)

Affair-Proof Your Marriage

Ecclesiastes 10:8

Heart to heart: In what ways can you affair-proof your marriage?

WEEK TWENTY TWO

Protecting Your Marriage (Part 2)
Letting Go of Past Relationships

Song of Solomon 2:15

Heart to heart: What past and/or harmful relationships do you need to let go of?

WEEK TWENTY THREE

Protecting Your Marriage (Part 3)

Laying Aside the Weight

Hebrews 12:1

Heart to heart: Are there any past experiences hindering your marriage relationship?

WEEK TWENTY FOUR

Protecting Your Marriage (Part 4)
Guard Your Heart

Proverbs 4:23

Heart to heart: In what ways do you need to guard your heart and protect your marriage?

WEEK TWENTY FIVE

Choose Life

Romans 6:23

Heart to heart: What temptations do you need to overcome in your marriage?

WEEK TWENTY SIX

Marriage Robber (Part 1)
Strife

John 10:10

Heart to heart: How do you resolve conflict? Is it healthy?

WEEK TWENTY SEVEN

Marriage Robber (Part 2)
Selfishness

Philippians 2:3-4

Heart to heart: In what ways have you been selfish in your marriage? What can you do to make amends?

WEEK TWENTY EIGHT

Marriage Robber (Part 3)
The Enemy Within - Negative Thoughts

Philippians 4:8

Heart to heart: What negative thoughts about your spouse and marriage do you need to let go of?

WEEK TWENTY NINE

The Blame Game

Matthew 7:5

Heart to heart: In what ways do I play the blame game in our marriage?
(Reflect on your own and discuss)

WEEK THIRTY

Making Every Day Count

Ephesians 5:15-16

Heart to heart: In what ways is the enemy stealing your time with each other? What can you do to avoid the little things that become bones of contention?

WEEK THIRTY ONE

Investments in Your Marriage (Part 1)
A Threefold Cord

Ecclesiastes 4:9-12

Heart to heart: In what ways can you better support each other?

WEEK THIRTY TWO

Investments in Your Marriage (Part 2)

Prayer: The Best Gift You Can Give

Ecclesiastes 4:9-12

Heart to heart: Share your prayer needs with each other. Both the small and big things. Pray for each other.

WEEK THIRTY THREE

Investments in Your Marriage (Part 3)
Praying Together

Ecclesiastes 4:9-12

Heart to heart: In what ways can you improve your prayer times together?

WEEK THIRTY FOUR

Keeping the Flames of Love Alive

Song of Solomon 8:6-7

Heart to heart: What can you do to keep igniting passion and romance in your marriage?

WEEK THIRTY FIVE

Deposits in Your Love Bank (Part 1)

Galatians 6:9

Heart to heart: In what ways can you put love deposits into your marriage?

WEEK THIRTY SIX

Deposits in Your Love Bank (Part 2)

Proverbs 19:11

Heart to heart: Are you holding any hurt against your spouse?
Is there anything you need to share with each other?

WEEK THIRTY SEVEN

Deposits in Your Love Bank (Part 3)

Proverbs 17:9

Heart to heart: Identify and discuss any issue you need to ask or offer forgiveness for.

WEEK THIRTY EIGHT

Deposits in Your Love Bank (Part 4)

I Corinthians 13:4

Heart to heart: In what ways do you need to be more patient with your spouse?

WEEK THIRTY NINE

Enjoying each other

Proverbs 5:18

Heart to heart: In what ways can you celebrate your love for each other?

WEEK FORTY

Speaking the Truth in Love

Ephesians 4:15,29

Heart to heart: In what ways do you need to change your communication style to reflect truth and grace?

WEEK FORTY ONE

Responding to Change (Part 1)

Ecclesiastes 3:1-8

Heart to heart: How are you responding to changes in your marriage journey? What changes do you need to accept in each other?

WEEK FORTY TWO

Responding to Change (Part 2)

Ecclesiastes 3:1-8

Heart to heart: What mindset do you have about your marriage that needs to change?

WEEK FORTY THREE

Blended Gifts

Genesis 5:2

Heart to heart: List five differences between you and your spouse. How can these differences make your marriage more balanced and complete?

WEEK FORTY FOUR

Money Talks

Luke 14:28-29

Heart to heart: How are you building financial intimacy in your marriage?

WEEK FORTY FIVE

Knowing Me, Knowing You

Colossians 3:12

Heart to heart: What does your spouse need from you at this time? Ask each other.

WEEK FORTY SIX

Expressions of Love (Part 1)

Song of Solomon 8:7

Heart to heart: In what ways can you show commitment to your spouse?

WEEK FORTY SEVEN

Expressions of Love (Part 2)

Song of Solomon 8:7

Heart to heart: Discuss your love language with each other. How can you make your spouse feel deeply loved this week?

WEEK FORTY EIGHT

A Godly Heritage

Proverbs 14:26

Heart to heart: How can you help your children build their relationship with God?

WEEK FORTY NINE

Your Legacy

Ephesians 6:4

Heart to heart: How would your children describe your marriage?

WEEK FIFTY

Praying for Your Child(ren)

James 5:16b

Heart to heart: How can you pray for and with your child(ren)?

WEEK FIFTY ONE

Lean on me

Proverbs 13:20

Heart to heart: Who are those couples around you whose influence strengthen your marriage?

WEEK FIFTY TWO

Treasure in Heavenly Places

Matthew 6:19-21

Heart to heart: How can your marriage be a godly influence to those around you?

Printed in Poland
by Amazon Fulfillment
Poland Sp. z o.o., Wrocław

57962131R00063

NATIONAL GEOGRAPHIC
School Publishing

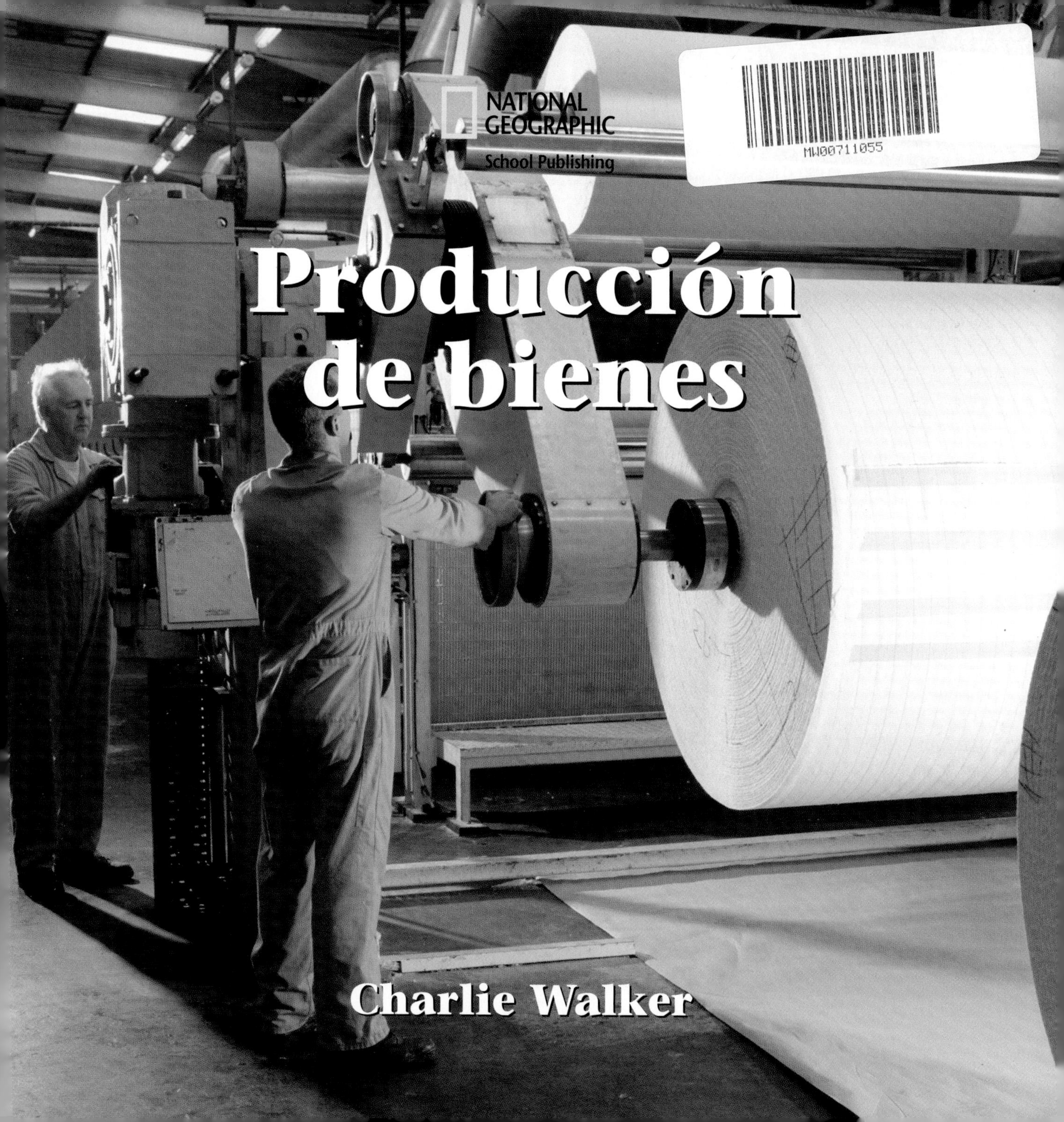

Producción de bienes

Charlie Walker

PICTURE CREDITS
Cover, 1, 4 (left below and right), 5 (right below), 7 (above and left below), 8, 9 (below), 10, 11 (right and below), 13 (above and right), 14, 17 (above right), 19 (above and below), 20 (left below), 20 (right center and right below), Photolibrary.com; 3 (left), 7 (right below), 12, 17 (below), 21 (right below), Getty Images; 4 (left above), 9 (right), 11 (above), 13 (below), 16 (right), 18, 20 (center below), APL/Corbis; 5 (right above), Alaska Stock LLC/Alamy; 6 and 16 (left) , Helene Rogers/Alamy; 15 (above), Jeff Greenberg/Alamy; 15 (below), John Powell Photographer/Alamy; 9 (above), CSIRO; 17 (left above and right) Dorling Kindersley.

Produced through the worldwide resources of the National Geographic Society, John M. Fahey, Jr., President and Chief Executive Officer; Gilbert M. Grosvenor, Chairman of the Board.

PREPARED BY NATIONAL GEOGRAPHIC SCHOOL PUBLISHING
Steve Mico, Executive Vice President and Publisher, Children's Books and Education Publishing Group; Marianne Hiland, Editor in Chief; Lynnette Brent, Executive Editor; Michael Murphy and Barbara Wood, Senior Editors; Nicole Rouse, Editor; Bea Jackson, Design Director; David Dumo, Art Director; Shanin Glenn, Designer; Margaret Sidlosky, Illustrations Director; Matt Wascavage, Manager of Publishing Services; Sean Philpotts, Production Manager.

SPANISH LANGUAGE VERSION PREPARED BY NATIONAL GEOGRAPHIC SCHOOL PUBLISHING GROUP
Sheron Long, CEO; Sam Gesumaria, President; Fran Downey, Vice President and Publisher; Margaret Sidlosky, Director of Design and Illustrations; Paul Osborn, Senior Editor; Sean Philpotts, Project Manager; Lisa Pergolizzi, Production Manager.

MANUFACTURING AND QUALITY MANAGEMENT
Christopher A. Liedel, Chief Financial Officer; George Bounelis, Vice President; Clifton M. Brown III, Director.

BOOK DEVELOPMENT
Ibis for Kids Australia Pty Limited.

SPANISH LANGUAGE TRANSLATION
Tatiana Acosta/Guillermo Gutiérrez

SPANISH LANGUAGE BOOK DEVELOPMENT
Navta Associates, Inc.

Published by the National Geographic Society
Washington, D.C. 20036-4688

ISBN: 978-0-7362-3861-8

Printed in Canada

12 11 10 09 08

10 9 8 7 6 5 4 3 2 1

Contenido

Pensar y conversar

Hablen sobre estos productos o bienes. ¿Con qué cosas de la naturaleza se hicieron?

¿De dónde vienen los bienes?

Muchos de los **bienes** que necesitamos y deseamos se hacen con **materias primas** que están en la naturaleza.

La cerámica se hace con arcilla. La arcilla viene de la tierra.

La ropa de lana
se hace con
lana de oveja.

La ropa de algodón se hace
con plantas de algodón.

Casi todo el papel se hace
con madera de los árboles.

El helado se hace
con leche de vaca.

De la oveja a los calcetines de lana

La lana de oveja es una materia prima. La lana se usa para hacer muchas cosas, entre ellas ropa. La lana pasa por muchas etapas para convertirse en artículos de lana.

A las ovejas les sale un pelaje de lana. Una vez al año, se les corta la lana. A esto se le llama esquilar.

La lana se lleva a una **fábrica.** Allí, se carda en enormes **máquinas** para alisarla.

La lana se transforma en hilo y se tiñe de diferentes colores.

Con el hilo se tejen artículos de lana, como estos calcetines.

Del algodonero a la camiseta de algodón

Un algodonero es una materia prima. El algodón se usa para hacer muchas cosas, entre ellas ropa. El algodón pasa por muchas etapas para convertirse en artículos de algodón.

En el algodonero brotan unas cápsulas llenas de algodón. Para **cosechar** el algodón, los agricultores usan desmotadoras de algodón.

El algodón se envía a una fábrica. Allí, se limpia y se carda para alisarlo.

Una máquina trenza el algodón para hacer hilo.

Con el hilo se teje tela. Con la tela se hacen artículos de algodón, como esta camiseta.

De la madera al papel

La madera de los árboles es una materia prima. La madera se usa para hacer muchas cosas, entre ellas papel. La madera pasa por muchas etapas para convertirse en papel.

Las virutas de madera se mezclan con agua para hacer pulpa. La pulpa se pone en enormes rodillos calientes para que se seque.

Los grandes rollos de papel se cortan en hojas de papel.

El papel se usa para hacer artículos como este libro.

De las vacas lecheras al helado

La leche de las vacas es una materia prima. Las personas beben leche y la usan para hacer muchas cosas, entre ellas helados. La leche pasa por muchas etapas para convertirse en helado.

Las vacas **producen** leche. Por lo general, las vacas se ordeñan con máquinas.

La leche se envía a fábricas. Allí, se mezcla con otros ingredientes y se congela para hacer helado.

El helado se envasa en tarrinas.

La gente compra helado y se lo come.

De la arcilla a las vasijas

La arcilla de la tierra es una materia prima. La arcilla se usa para hacer muchas cosas, entre ellas cerámica. La arcilla pasa por muchas etapas para convertirse en cerámica.

La arcilla se extrae de debajo del suelo. Cuando se moja, se vuelve suave y se le puede dar forma.

Hay distintas maneras de trabajar la arcilla. Se le suele dar forma en un torno de alfarero.

Los objetos de arcilla se meten en hornos calientes especiales. El calor endurece la arcilla.

Con la arcilla se hacen muchos **productos** útiles y bellos.

De los árboles a las llantas

El látex del árbol de caucho es una materia prima. Con el látex se hace caucho, que se puede usar para hacer muchas cosas, entre ellas llantas. El látex pasa por muchas etapas para convertirse en llantas.

El árbol de caucho produce un líquido pegajoso llamado látex. El látex se recoge en los árboles.

El látex se pasa por grandes rodillos que le exprimen el agua y lo aplastan para hacer láminas. Estas láminas se secan y se empaquetan.

El látex se envía a fábricas. Se mezcla con productos químicos y se usa para hacer llantas.

Muchas clases de vehículos, entre ellos los autos, usan llantas de caucho.

Usar lo que aprendieron

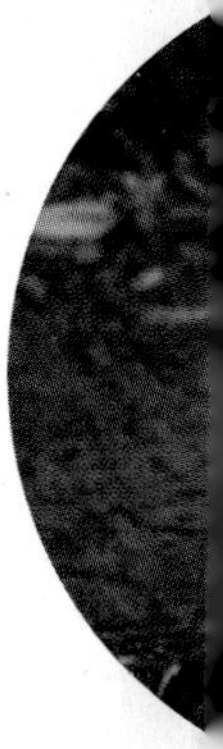

¿Qué materias primas se usaron para producir los bienes que se muestran abajo?

bienes

cosechar

fábrica

máquina

materia prima

producto

Glosario

CONCEPTO CLAVE

bienes (página 6)
Cualquier producto que puede venderse
Muchos de los bienes que necesitamos y deseamos se hacen con materias primas que están en la naturaleza.

CONCEPTO CLAVE

cosechar (página 10)
Recoger la cosecha de algo
Los agricultores cosechan el algodón con desmotadoras de algodón.

CONCEPTO CLAVE

fábrica (página 9)
Lugar donde las materias primas son procesadas
La lana se carda y se transforma en hilo en una fábrica.

CONCEPTO CLAVE

máquina (página 9)
Algo que tiene muchas partes que funcionan juntas para realizar un trabajo
Una máquina trenza el algodón para hacer hilo.

CONCEPTO CLAVE

materia prima (página 6)
Cualquier material de la naturaleza que se usa para hacer productos
Los trabajadores deben seguir una serie de pasos para transformar una materia prima en un producto terminado que puede venderse.

producir (página 14)
Transformar materias primas en productos terminados
La leche se usa para producir helado.

CONCEPTO CLAVE

producto (página 17)
Algo que se fabrica o cultiva para el consumo humano
Los productos de cerámica se hacen con arcilla.

Índice